We the People

Founding Documents

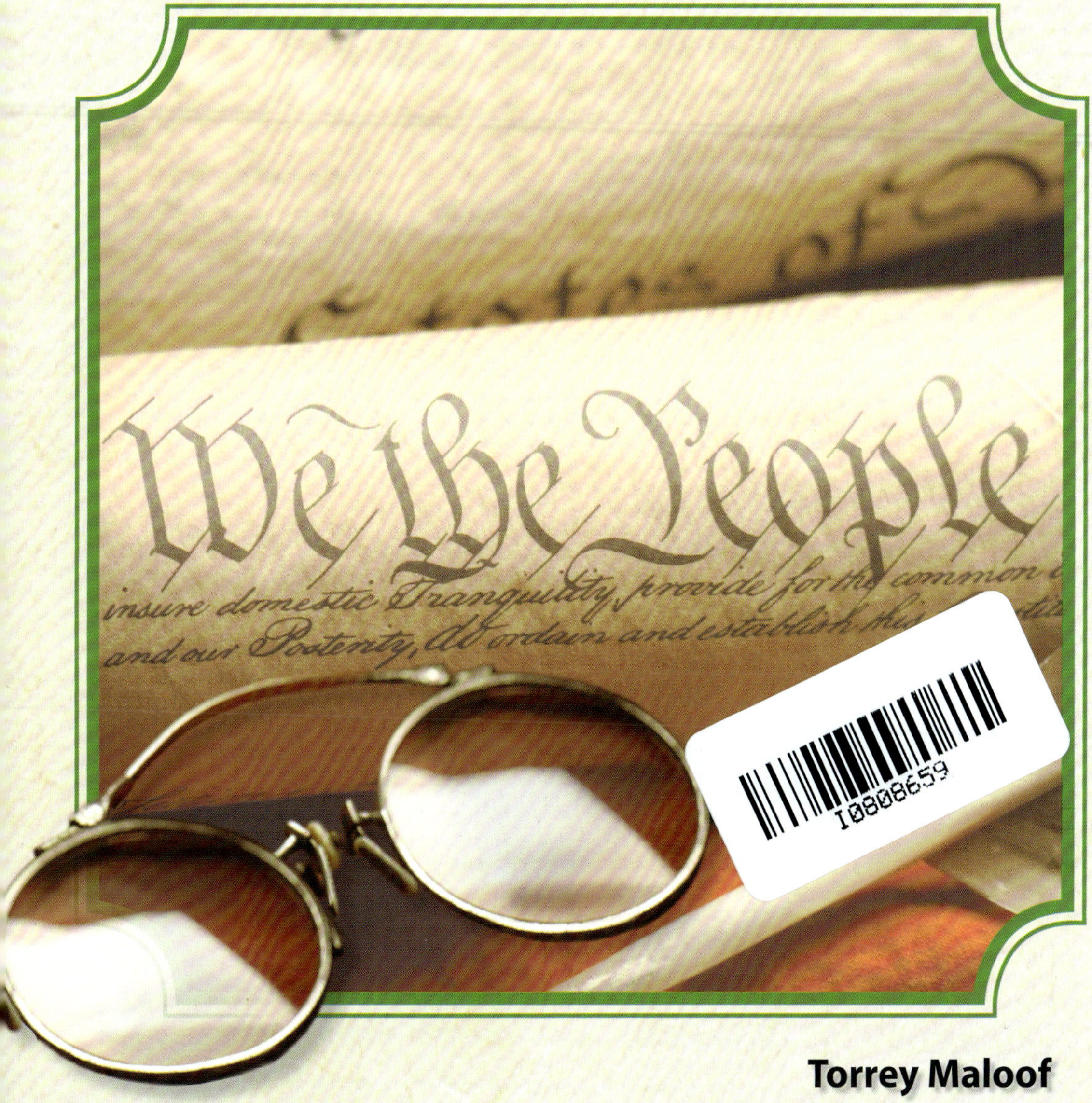

Torrey Maloof

Consultants

Katie Blomquist, M.Ed.
Fairfax County Public Schools

Nicholas Baker, Ed.D.
Supervisor of Curriculum and Instruction
Colonial School District, DE

Publishing Credits

Rachelle Cracchiolo, M.S.Ed., *Publisher*
Conni Medina, M.A.Ed., *Managing Editor*
Emily R. Smith, M.A.Ed., *Series Developer*
Diana Kenney, M.A.Ed., NBCT, *Content Director*
Johnson Nguyen, *Multimedia Designer*
Torrey Maloof, *Editor*

Image Credits: pp. 2–3, 6 LOC [LC-DIG-highsm-15713]; pp. 4, 17 Granger, NYC; p. 5 LOC [LC-USZ62-3795]; p. 7 National Archives and Records Administration; p. 8 LOC [LC-USZC4-9904]; p. 9 U.S. Capitol/ Public Domain; pp.10, 11, 12, 13 North Wind Picture Archives; p. 11 American Treasures of the Library of Congress; p. 16 LOC [us0048]; pp. 16, 18–19 Wikimedia Commons/Public Domain; p. 18 LOC [LC-USZ62-70508]; p. 20 JSP Studios/Alamy; pp. 22–23 Sonya N. Hebert/ White House; p. 24 LOC [LC-DIG-ppmsca-37229]; p. 26 Chuck Pefley/ Alamy; p. 27 (top) National Archives, General Records of the U.S. Government, (middle) The Abraham Lincoln Papers at the Library of Congress, Manuscript Division, (bottom) NARA [26080947]; pp. 28–29 Michael Ventura/Alamy; LOC [LC-DIG-ppmsca-37229]; all other images from iStock and/or Shutterstock.

Library of Congress Cataloging-in-Publication Data

Names: Maloof, Torrey, author.
Title: We the people : founding documents / Torrey Maloof.
Description: Huntington Beach, CA : Teacher Created Materials, 2017. | Includes index. | Audience: Grades 4-6.
Identifiers: LCCN 2015051150 (print) | LCCN 2016018758 (ebook) | ISBN 9781493830848 (pbk.) | ISBN 9781480756861 (eBook)
Subjects: LCSH: United States--Politics and government--1775-1783--Sources--Juvenile literature. | United States--Politics and government--1783-1791--Sources--Juvenile literature.
Classification: LCC E210 .M13 2017 (print) | LCC E210 (ebook) | DDC 973.3--dc23
LC record available at https://lccn.loc.gov/2015051150

Teacher Created Materials
5301 Oceanus Drive
Huntington Beach, CA 92649-1030
http://www.tcmpub.com

ISBN 978-1-4938-3084-8

Printed by: 590835
Printed in: China

Table of Contents

Powerful Words

It's 1963. Over 200,000 people are packed into the National Mall. It is a warm summer day—too warm for some. These folks can be seen cooling their feet in the reflecting pool. A man stands in front of the Lincoln Memorial. He gives a speech about his dreams. In it he states, "I have a dream that one day this nation will rise up and live out the true meaning of its creed: 'We hold these truths to be self-evident, that *all men are created equal.*' " Dr. Martin Luther King Jr. quotes the Declaration of Independence. He uses it to convey his thoughts on equality and freedom. As he speaks, a large man made of marble sits behind him. That man is Abraham Lincoln.

Martin Luther King Jr. delivers his famous "I Have a Dream" speech.

Let's go back another 100 years. It is now 1863. President Lincoln stands on a battlefield in Gettysburg. He gives a speech. His speech is also about equality and freedom. In the speech he says, "Four score and seven years ago, our fathers brought forth, on this continent, a new nation, conceived in Liberty, and dedicated to the proposition that *all men are created equal.*" Like King, Lincoln references the Declaration.

Abraham Lincoln delivers the Gettysburg Address.

Declaration Author

Thomas Jefferson was the main author of the Declaration of Independence.

The founding documents are on display at the National Archives in Washington, DC.

The Declaration of Independence is one of the founding **documents** of the United States. These documents are the important texts on which the country is built. These texts changed the course of history. They tell the story of America. They contain the ideals for which America stands. They stand for freedom. They stand for change. So what are these documents?

As mentioned, there is the Declaration of Independence. This letter to the king of Great Britain ignited the American Revolution. It gave birth to a new country. There are the **Articles** of **Confederation**. They served as the nation's first attempt at a **constitution**. They set a young nation's rules for its new government. Then, there is the Constitution that we know today. It explains how the country and its government should work. And lastly, there is the Bill of **Rights**. This section of the Constitution protects the personal freedoms of all Americans.

Everyday English

The founding documents were written in everyday, simple English. But you wouldn't know it by reading them! Today, we find the language tough to read. This is because, over time, the English language has changed a great deal.

People read the founding documents in Washington, DC.

The language of these documents can be difficult to understand. We do not write and speak in the same way as the Founding Fathers. But we must not let that stop us from reading and analyzing these texts. It is important to know the meaning and purpose of each of these documents; for without them, America would not be what it is today.

Declaration of Independence

It's the summer of 1776. After much debate, the **Continental Congress** has decided it is time to declare independence from Great Britain. A special document is needed. It will explain all the reasons the colonists want and deserve freedom. Thomas Jefferson will write it. Then, committee will review it. It will be called the Declaration of Independence.

The Declaration Committee reviews a draft of the Declaration of Independence.

The Continental Congress signs the Declaration of Independence in 1776.

The first sentence of the Declaration states its purpose. Jefferson made it clear that the time had come for the two nations to "separate." He wrote that the "Laws of Nature and Nature's God" give colonists the right to break free from Great Britain. Jefferson said that he would list reasons for this forced separation later in the document.

The next sentence is the most famous. It is frequently quoted. It inspires people around the world. Jefferson wrote, "All men are created equal." He explained that *everyone* should have the same basic rights. They should have the right to live freely and happily.

ALL Men

At the time the Declaration was written, **slavery** was legal. Benjamin Banneker was a free black man. In 1791, Banneker wrote to Jefferson. He reminded Jefferson of his famous words about *all men* in hopes that he would join the fight to end slavery. But sadly, slavery continued for many more years.

Benjamin Banneker

Jefferson went on to write that the government's power rests in the hands of the people. The government's main job is to protect the people's basic rights. If it does not do its job, then the people can "throw off such [a] government" and form a new one.

Next, Jefferson wrote about King George III. He boldly proclaimed that the king of Great Britain had committed "absolute **tyranny**." He took away the basic rights of the people in the colonies. This was their reason for declaring independence. To prove his point, Jefferson composed a long list of complaints against the king.

The list showed how the king put colonists in danger and cost them money. Jefferson noted that the king refused to pass laws that would help colonists. He taxed them without their approval. He stopped the colonies from trading with other countries. The king denied people trial by jury. He forced colonists to keep British troops. The king said that he would not protect colonists from enemies. The list went on and on.

Colonists throw British tea into Boston Harbor to protest British taxes.

Colonists speak out against unfair British taxes.

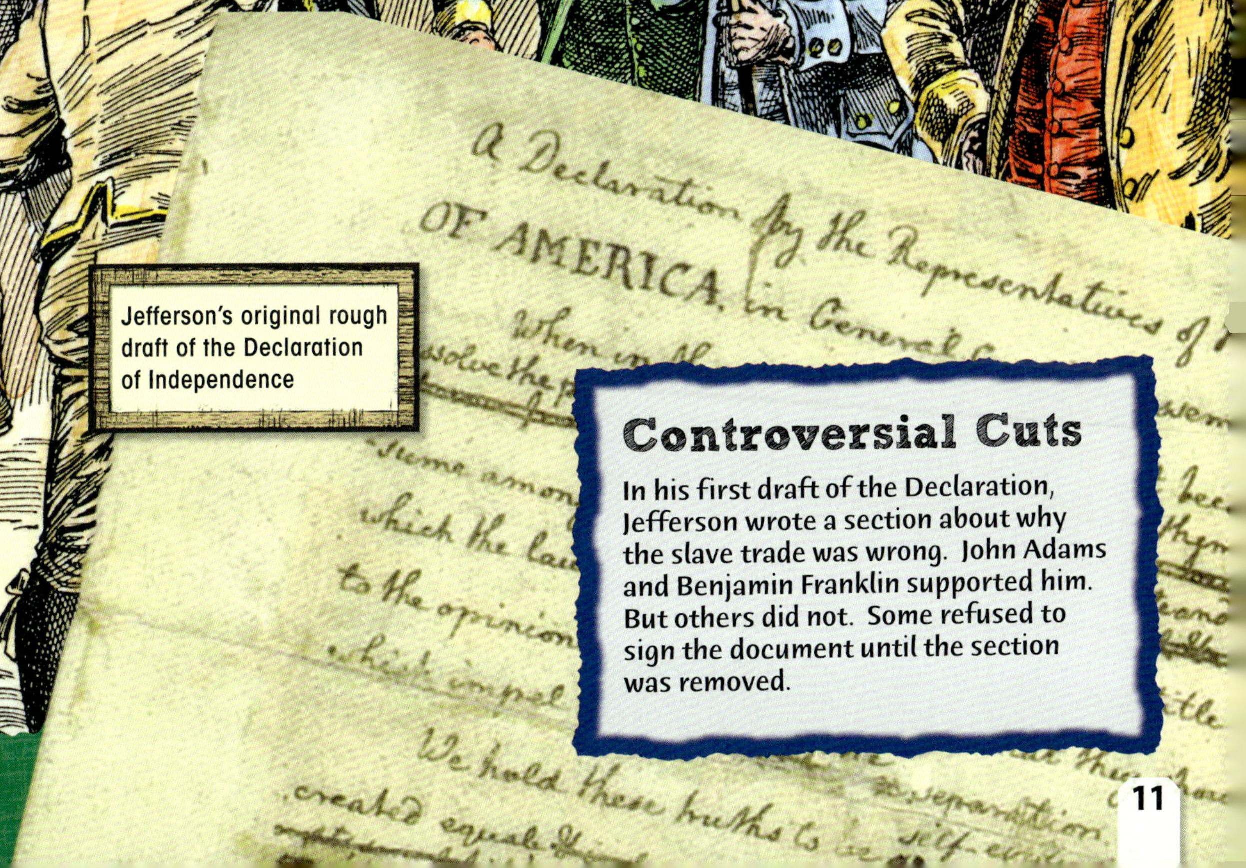

Jefferson's original rough draft of the Declaration of Independence

Controversial Cuts

In his first draft of the Declaration, Jefferson wrote a section about why the slave trade was wrong. John Adams and Benjamin Franklin supported him. But others did not. Some refused to sign the document until the section was removed.

Colonists listen as the Declaration of Independence is read for the first time.

After the list of **grievances**, Jefferson explained that this was not the colonists' first attempt to inform the king of the problems they faced. They tried many times. But the king ignored all their requests. Jefferson stated that they also asked the British government and its citizens for help. These pleas were disregarded, as well. He wrote, "They too have been deaf to the voice of justice."

Jefferson wrote to the king that the colonies had "united" together as one. They had formed a new country—the United States of America. It would be made up of "free and independent states." He then declared that these states would be "**absolved** from all **allegiance** to the British crown." They would no longer be tied to the British government. They could wage war on their own. They could make peace agreements by themselves. They could trade with countries of their choice. The United States had publicly announced its independence.

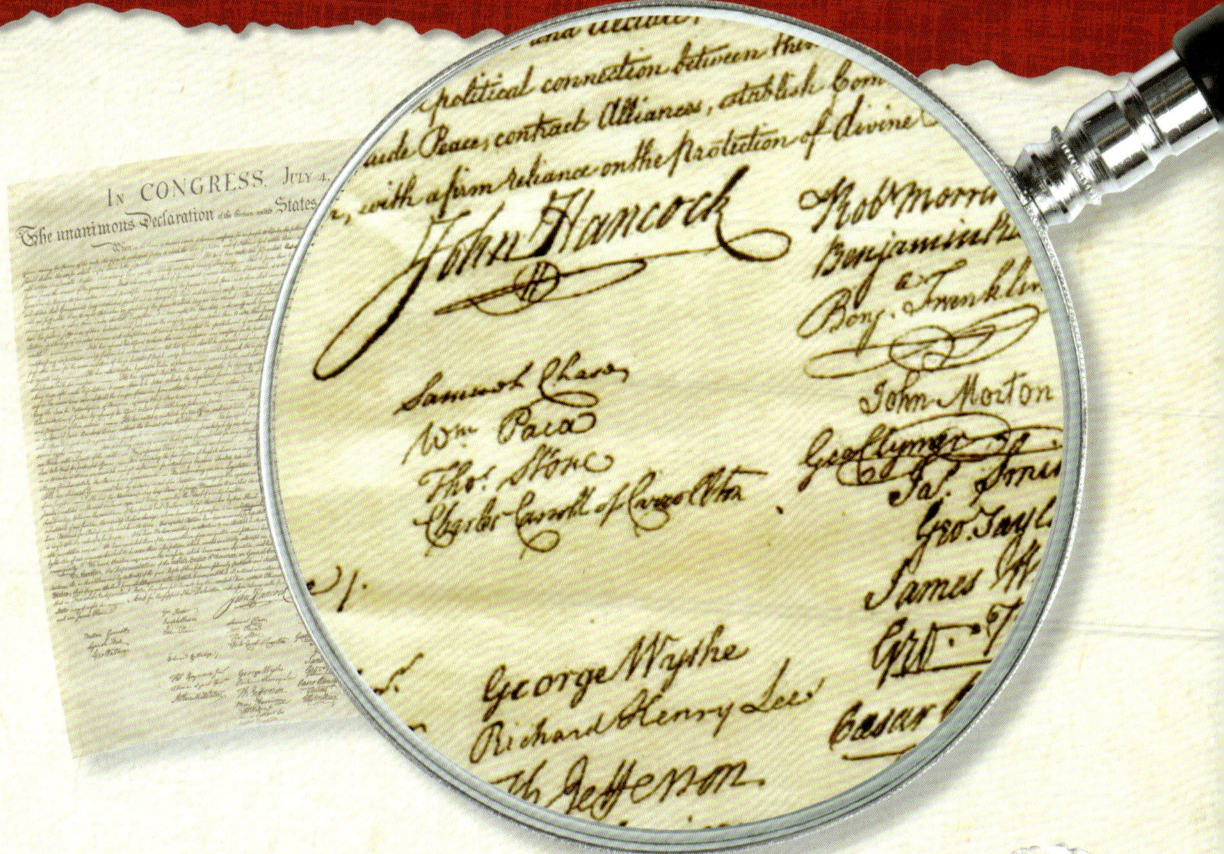

The letter concludes with 56 signatures. Signing this document was a brave thing to do. If the United States had not won the American Revolution, these men could have been hanged for **treason**.

The Declaration serves as an inspiration for many around the world. It shows that everyone can demand equal rights.

Sign Here

As president of the Continental Congress, John Hancock was the first to sign the Declaration. Legend has it that he made his signature extra large so that the king could read it without his glasses. But others point out that Hancock used this same bulky signature on most of his documents.

Articles of Confederation

Now that the United States had declared its independence, it needed to form a government. It needed a national government that would unite individual states under one set of rules. The Congress decided to write a constitution. It would be the first set of rules for the new nation. These rules would be called the Articles of Confederation.

The Congress faced a big problem while drafting the Articles. Some leaders felt that there needed to be a strong national government—one that could tax its citizens and raise money for the war against Great Britain. But others felt that a strong national government would take away the rights of citizens. They feared it would be too much like the British government. These **delegates** wanted each state to have more power than the national government.

There was also the problem of how much power each state would have. Would larger states have more power? Or would all states have equal power? Many tough decisions had to be made. And they needed to be made quickly!

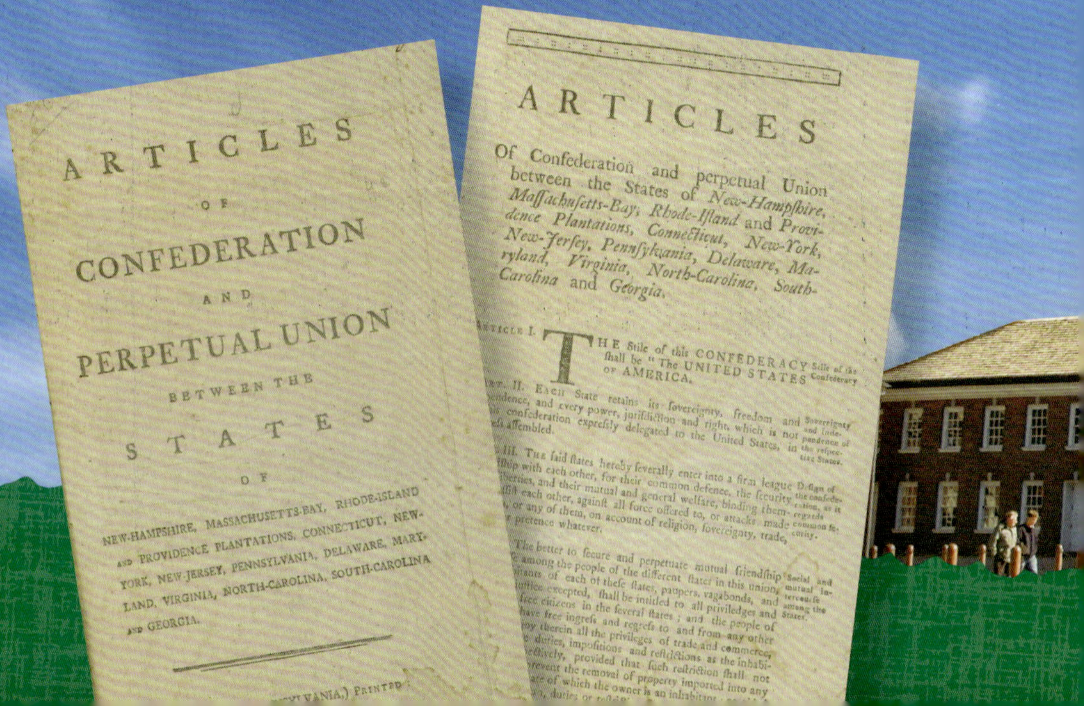

A Sweltering Summer

Secrecy was of the utmost importance during meetings of the Congress. Delegates needed to freely speak their minds. Thus, windows were kept shut. Heavy curtains were drawn closed. The meeting rooms were hot and stuffy, but the Founders, in their heavy formal clothes, pressed on.

The Congress met in Independence Hall in Philadelphia.

On November 15, 1777, the Congress agreed on and adopted the Articles of Confederation. Each state would keep its freedom and independence. It would have control over itself. But each state would also enter into a "firm league of friendship." They would help each other and work together to defend the country against attacks.

The Articles stated that there would be no president of the United States, but rather a president of Congress. This president would have no power. He could not join the meetings. He could only lead the meetings. He would not even be allowed to vote. Delegates would choose a new president each year.

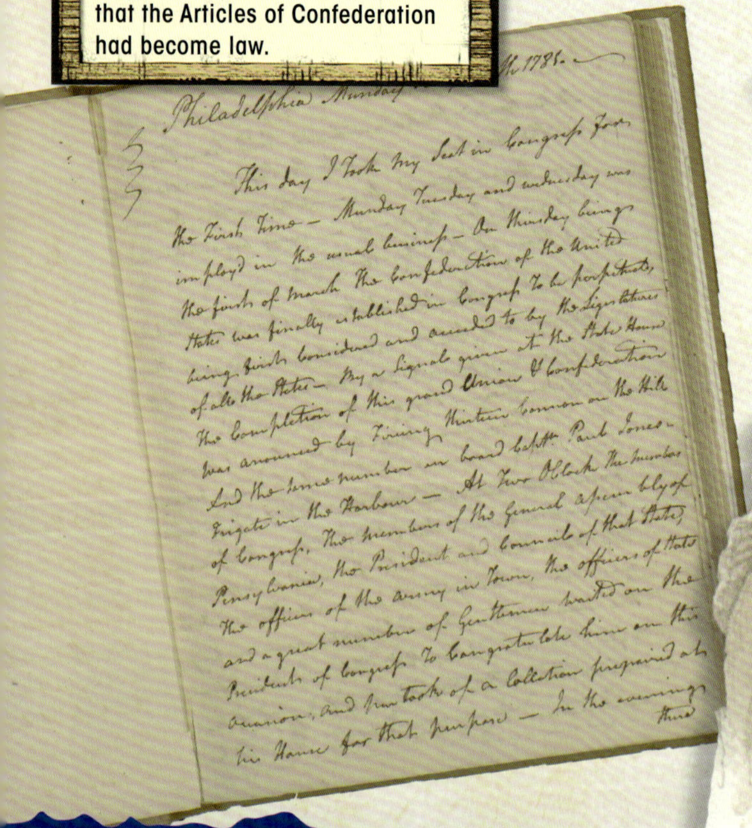

Philadelphia Monday ... 1781 —

This day I took my Seat in Congress for the First Time — Monday Tuesday and Wednesday was imployed in the usual business — On Thursday being the first of March The Confederation of the United States was finally established in Congress to be perpetual, being first considered and acceded to by the Signatures of all the States — By a Signal given at the State House the Completion of this grand Union & Confederation was announced by Firing Thirteen Cannon on the Hills And the same number on board Capt. Paul Jones's Frigate in the Harbour — At Two OClock The members of Congress, The members of the General Assembly of Pensylvania, the President and Council of that State, The officers of the army in Town, the officers of State and a great number of Gentlemen waited on the President of Congress To Congratulate him on this Occasion; and partook of a Collation prepared at his House for that purpose — In the evening there

This diary entry from Delaware delegate, Thomas Rodney, explains that the Articles of Confederation had become law.

Samuel Huntington was the first president of Congress under the Articles of Confederation.

The Articles had some strengths. It protected states' rights, and it got the new country through the American Revolution. But it had many weaknesses. Congress had very limited power. There were no national courts. Congress could not tax citizens; it could only ask states for money. The size and population of each state did not matter. They all had equal power. Each state had one vote in Congress.

This all resulted in a very weak central government. Problems began to arise. The country was in trouble. By 1787, many agreed that it was time to make some changes—big changes!

This cartoon from the 20th century shows how the Articles of Confederation was one step towards the writing of the U.S. Constitution.

Money Madness

The national government was unable to collect enough money to fund the war. To make matters worse, states used different types of money. Some states wouldn't accept money from other states. All this was because the Articles didn't include rules about money.

Continental dollars from 1776

Constitution

In May, delegates from 12 of the 13 states met in Philadelphia. They met to fix the Articles of Confederation. The 55 delegates agreed to work together. They wanted to improve the laws of the United States. These men would later be known as the Framers. Because instead of mending the Articles, they created a new document. They framed, or wrote, the U.S. Constitution.

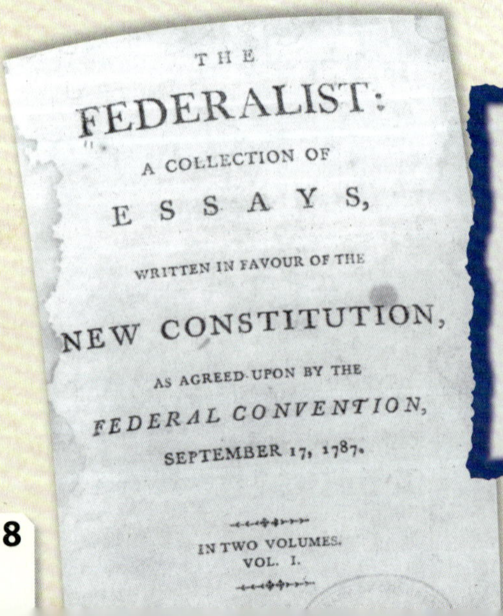

THE
FEDERALIST:
A COLLECTION OF
ESSAYS,
WRITTEN IN FAVOUR OF THE
NEW CONSTITUTION,
AS AGREED UPON BY THE
FEDERAL CONVENTION,
SEPTEMBER 17, 1787.
IN TWO VOLUMES.
VOL. I.

Why the Change?

Some people complained about changes that were being made as the Constitution was authored. So Alexander Hamilton, James Madison, and John Jay wrote letters explaining why the changes were good for the government. These letters came to be known as the Federalist Papers.

The Constitution is signed on September 17, 1787.

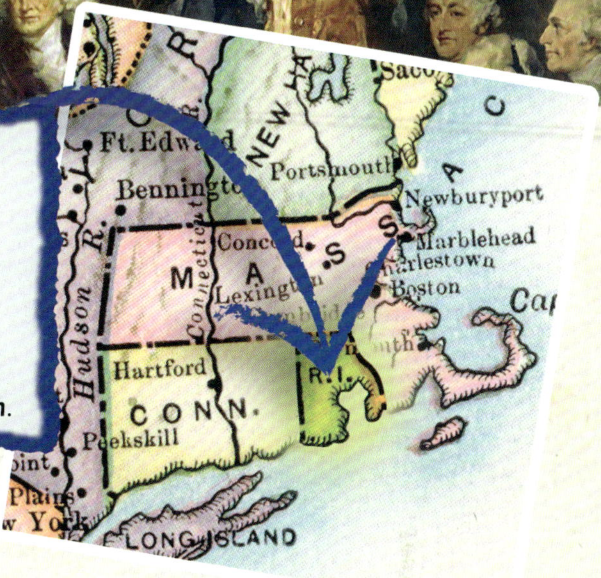

No Shows

Rhode Island did not want to change the Articles of Confederation. So they did not send any delegates to the meetings in Philadelphia. But, they later agreed to sign the Constitution once it was written.

Preamble

The Constitution begins with the Preamble. It is an introduction. It is 52 words long. It explains the purpose of the Constitution. The first three words of the Preamble—*We the People*—are some of the most powerful words in the document. These words refer to each and every citizen in the United States. They make it clear that the power of the U.S. government rests in the hands of its citizens. It is the people that give the government power, not the other way around. The Preamble goes on to explain that the Constitution will strengthen the weaknesses of the Articles. It is meant "to form a more perfect Union." It will do this by creating fair laws and keeping the peace. And it will promote the well-being and freedom of all U.S. citizens.

Articles

Following the Preamble, there are the seven articles, or sections. They describe how the government should run the country. The Framers divided the government into three branches, or parts. They did this to keep one branch from having too much power. It created a system of checks and balances. This is outlined in the first three articles.

Article I talks about the legislative branch. Its job is to create laws. Congress is part of this branch. Congress consists of the Senate and the House of **Representatives**. The Constitution explains that each state has two senators. But the number of representatives varies. That depends on how many people live in a state. States with more people have more members in the House.

Article II explains the executive branch. Its job is to enforce the laws. The president of the United States is the leader of this branch. The Constitution contains rules about who can be president. This branch includes the vice president, the president's **cabinet**, and members of the military.

Article III is about the judicial branch. This is the **federal**, or national, court system. Its job is to interpret laws. The Constitution tells how federal judges are selected. It explains how the Supreme Court functions. This is the highest court in the United States.

Why Do We Vote on Tuesday?

In 1845, Congress chose the first Tuesday in November as Election Day. November was a good month because it was between the planting season and the harvest. Voting on a Tuesday gave people a day to travel, a day to vote, and a day to travel back home. They could do all of this without it interfering with market day or the three days of worship.

This man votes in an election.

Judicial Branch

- Can declare executive actions unconstitutional

Executive Branch

Carries out the Law

Executive Branch

- Appoints federal judges

Legislative Branch

- Can override a veto
- Can declare war on other countries
- Can remove president

Executive Branch

- Can propose laws
- Can veto, or reject, laws
- Can call special sessions of Congress

Judicial Branch

Interprets the Law

Legislative Branch

- Can remove judges
- Can overrule judicial decisions
- Approves appointments of federal judges

Legislative Branch

Makes the Law

Judicial Branch

- Can declare acts of Congress unconstitutional

President Barack Obama takes the oath of office in 2013.

The fourth article of the Constitution is about the states. It explains the duties each state has to the federal government. It also describes the obligations the federal government has to each state. And it talks about the relationship between states.

The fifth article is about **amendments**, or changes. The Framers understood that as the country grew, it would need to make changes to the Constitution. New amendments can be added. But there are rules! States can call a constitutional convention. Or two-thirds of the Senate or the House need to agree to the change. Then, states need to vote in favor of the change. This is how all the amendments have been added.

The sixth article reminds people that the Constitution is the "supreme Law of the Land." It is the highest law of the country. It explains that federal laws are higher than state and local laws. It also talks about **oaths**. It says that all members of the government must swear an oath to uphold the Constitution.

The seventh article is one sentence. It is the last one. It is about **ratifying** the Constitution. Ratifying is making something official through signing or voting. Nine of the 13 states had to ratify the Constitution to make it official. By 1790, all 13 states had approved the document.

Bill of Rights

"It has no declaration of rights!" cried George Mason of Virginia. Mason wanted a list of rights to be added to the Constitution. He said he "would sooner chop off his right hand" than sign the Constitution the way it was. Luckily for Mason's right hand, 10 amendments were added. They are known as the Bill of Rights. They protect the rights of all U.S. citizens.

The First Amendment is a powerful one. It safeguards personal freedoms. It says Americans can practice any religion freely and safely. They can also say whatever they like without having to be afraid. They have freedom of speech. Americans can even criticize their government without getting in trouble. The press has the right to speak freely, too. Whether it be a news program on television or an article online, the press can decide what stories it wants to tell. Lastly, it grants people the right to assemble. People can meet to talk about the country's problems. They can bring these problems to the public's attention.

There are nine more amendments. Do you know which one says Americans can own weapons? Do you know which ones protect people who have been accused of committing crimes? Study the graphic closely. Learn which rights each amendment protects.

These people exercise their First Amendment rights in 1963 by walking in the March on Washington for Jobs and Freedom.

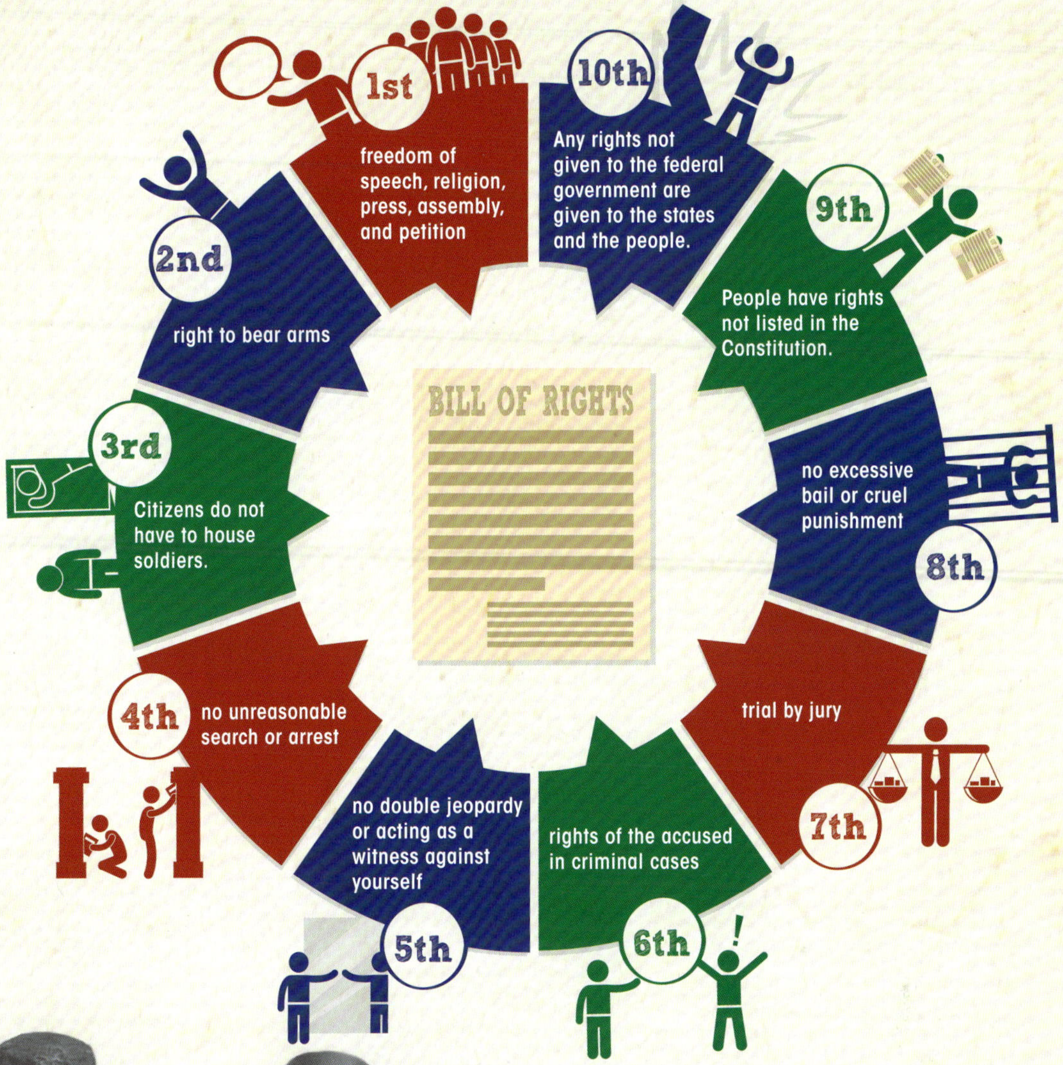

Even More Amendments

Over time, 17 more amendments were added to the Constitution. The 13th made slavery illegal. The 19th gave women the right to vote.

A Solid Foundation

There are many key texts besides the founding documents in America's history. Some documents changed the country. They helped it grow. They continue to guide it toward a better future. They inspire people and make them proud to be Americans. These documents include treaties, speeches, and songs. They include letters, transcripts, and photographs. Each one tells a story about the United States. But these documents would not exist if it were not for the founding documents.

The Declaration of Independence gave birth to the nation. It drove Americans to fight for their freedom and defend their liberties. The Articles of Confederation built a platform for a young country to stand on. It proved that a nation could be governed by its own people and not a king. Then came the Constitution. Not only does this document protect Americans' personal freedoms, it demonstrates how a country can grow and change without compromising its basic beliefs and principles.

All three of these documents are influential. They are bold. They are insightful. They remind people of the power of the pen. They show how small words can be combined to make big changes. "All men are created equal" and "we the people" were once written on a page and later changed the world.

People view the Declaration of Independence and the Constitution in Washington, DC.

Milestone Documents

Here are other important documents that shaped America. Do you know the history behind each one? It might be worth researching if you don't!

1800

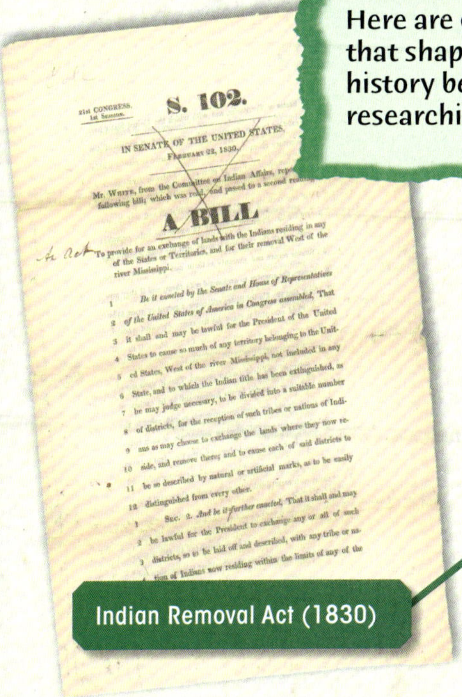

21st CONGRESS, 1st Session.

S. 102.

IN SENATE OF THE UNITED STATES, February 22, 1830.

Mr. White, from the Committee on Indian Affairs, rep... following bill; which was read, and passed to a second re...

A BILL

To provide for an exchange of lands with the Indians residing in any of the States or Territories, and for their removal West of the river Mississippi.

Be it enacted by the Senate and House of Representatives of the United States of America in Congress assembled, That it shall and may be lawful for the President of the United States to cause so much of any territory belonging to the United States, West of the river Mississippi, not included in any State, and to which the Indian title has been extinguished, as he may judge necessary, to be divided into a suitable number of districts, for the reception of such tribes or nations of Indians as may choose to exchange the lands where they now reside, and remove there; and to cause each of said districts to be so described by natural or artificial marks, as to be easily distinguished from every other.

Sec. 2. And be it further enacted, That it shall and may be lawful for the President to exchange any or all of such districts, so to be laid off and described, with any tribe or nation of Indians now residing within the limits of any of the

Indian Removal Act (1830)

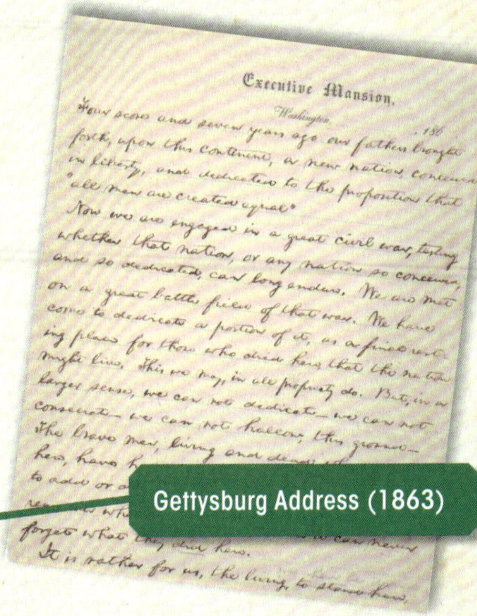

Executive Mansion,

Washington, 186

Four score and seven years ago our fathers brought forth, upon this continent, a new nation, conceived in liberty, and dedicated to the proposition that "all men are created equal"

Now we are engaged in a great civil war, testing whether that nation, or any nation so conceived, and so dedicated, can long endure. We are met on a great battle field of that war. We have come to dedicate a portion of it, as a final resting place for those who died here, that the nation might live, This we may, in all propriety do. But, in a larger sense, we can not dedicate—we can not consecrate—we can not hallow, this ground— The brave men, living and dead, who struggled here, have ...

to add or ...

... forget what they did here.

It is rather for us, the living, to stand here,

Gettysburg Address (1863)

1900

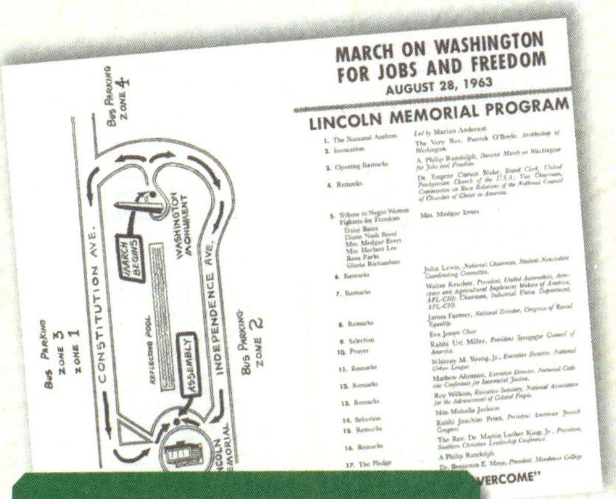

MARCH ON WASHINGTON FOR JOBS AND FREEDOM

AUGUST 28, 1963

LINCOLN MEMORIAL PROGRAM

1. The National Anthem — Led by Marian Anderson
2. Invocation — The Very Rev. Patrick O'Boyle, Archbishop of Washington
3. Opening Remarks — A. Philip Randolph, Director March on Washington for Jobs and Freedom
4. Remarks — Dr. Eugene Carson Blake
5. Tribute to Negro Women Fighters for Freedom — Mrs. Medgar Evers
6. Remarks — John Lewis
7. Remarks — Walter Reuther
8. Remarks — James Farmer
9. Selection — Eva Jessye Choir
10. Prayer — Rabbi Uri Miller
11. Remarks — Whitney M. Young, Jr.
12. Remarks — Mathew Ahmann
13. Remarks — Roy Wilkins
14. Selection — Miss Mahalia Jackson
15. Remarks — Rabbi Joachim Prinz
16. Remarks — The Rev. Dr. Martin Luther King, Jr.
17. The Pledge — A Philip Randolph

Dr. Benjamin E. Mays

...VERCOME"

March on Washington for Jobs and Freedom program (1963)

Rewrite It!

Read the Preamble to the Constitution on the right. Study the words closely. You may need to use a dictionary or thesaurus. Then, rewrite it in your own words. Be sure it means the same thing as the original. Share your version of the Preamble with your friends and family. Talk about what it means and why it is important.

The Preamble to the U.S. Constitution

"We the people of the United States, in Order to form a more perfect Union, establish Justice, insure domestic Tranquility, provide for the common defense, promote the general Welfare, and secure the Blessings of Liberty to ourselves and our Posterity, do ordain and establish this Constitution for the United States of America."

Glossary

absolved—set free from responsibility

allegiance—loyalty to a person, country, or group

amendments—changes to the words or meaning of a law or document

articles—separate parts of a legal document that deal with a single subject

cabinet—a group of people who give advice to the leader of a government

confederation—a government made up of several states in which those states have a lot of power over themselves

constitution—the system of beliefs and laws by which a country, state, or organization is governed

Continental Congress—meeting of colonial leaders to decide how to deal with Great Britain and to decide on laws

delegates—people chosen to speak for one of the colonies at the Continental Congress

documents—official papers that give information about something

federal—relating to the main government of the United States

grievances—statements that express unhappiness about something

oaths—formal promises to do something

ratifying—making official by signing or voting for it

representatives—people who act or speak for another person or group

rights—things that people should be allowed to have and do

slavery—being owned by another person and forced to work without pay

treason—the crime of attempting to overthrow the government of your own country or helping your country's enemy during war

tyranny—cruel and unfair treatment by people with power over others

Index

Your Turn!

Voting Rights

This photo shows people protesting in the 1963 March on Washington for Jobs and Freedom. The 15th amendment gave people of all races the right to vote. Women gained voting rights in 1920 when the 19th amendment was approved. So why might these people have been protesting for voting rights? Research the March on Washington to find out, and present your findings.